T0013743

Look Up High! Things That FLY

Victoria Allenby

pajamapress

Look up high!
Jet planes fly.
How? Where?
Look up there!
The jet plane
soars across
the sky

Look up high!
Gliders fly.
How? Where?
Look up there!
The glider
glides behind
a plane.

Look up high!
Airships fly.
How? Where?
Look up there!
The airship
floats below
the clouds.

Look up high!
Helicopters fly.
How? Where?
Look up there!
The helicopter
hovers above
the hill.

Look up high!
Space stations fly.
How? Where?
Look up there!
The space station
orbits around
the Earth.

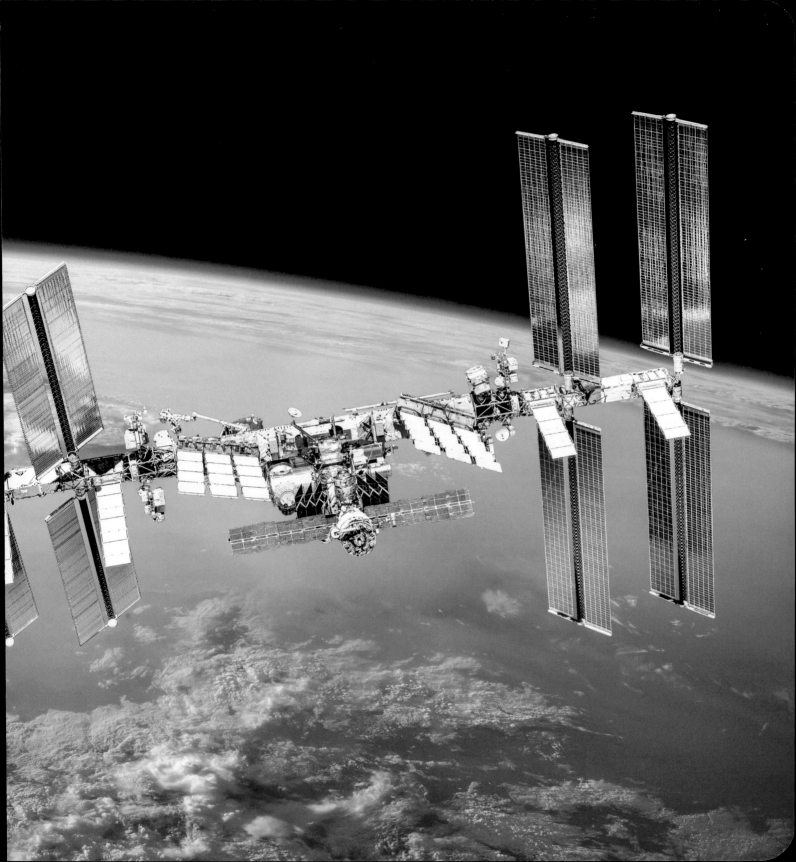

Look up high!
Water bombers fly.
How? Where?
Look up there!
The water bomber
swoops through
the smoke.

Look up high!
Toy planes fly.
How? Where?
Look up there!
The toy plane
zigzags left
and **right**.

Look up high!
Hot air balloons fly.
How? Where?
Look up there!
The hot air balloon
drifts between
the rocks.

Look up high!
People fly…

…**inside**
an airplane…
…**under**
a hang glider…
…**on top of**
a hovercraft…
…**beside**
a good friend.

How would **YOU** zoom across the sky?

Where is the airship in relation to the clouds?

The words that tell us are **prepositions**, and practicing them helps kids use language to talk about their world. Try these activities with your child:

1. Choose two small toys of different kinds. Help your child use them to model the prepositions you encounter in *Look Up High! Things That Fly* and describe them out loud: "The ball rolls **across** the book."

2. Take turns with the roles of an aircraft and an air traffic control officer, giving orders such as "Circle around the coffee table" and "Hover beside the chair."

3. Work with your child to make your own book by taking pictures and writing sentences to describe them: *Sophie runs **across** the lawn. Sophie hops **over** the line. Sophie crawls **into** the tunnel.*

4. Play a preposition version of I Spy during a walk or a car ride: "I spy with my little eye...a dog walking **in front of** a boy."

How else can you act out the most common prepositions?

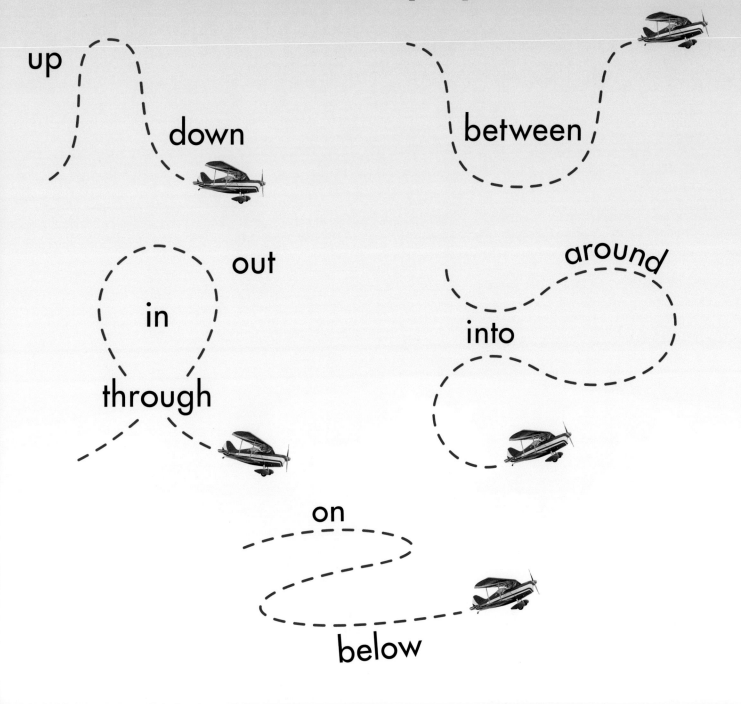

up

down

between

out

around

in

into

through

on

below

First published in Canada and the United States in 2023

Text copyright © 2023 Victoria Allenby
This edition copyright © 2023 Pajama Press Inc.
This is a first edition.
10 9 8 7 6 5 4 3 2 1

All rights reserved. No part of this publication may be reproduced, stored in a retrieval system or transmitted, in any form or by any means, without the prior written consent of the publisher or a licence from The Canadian Copyright Licensing Agency (Access Copyright). For an Access Copyright licence, visit www.accesscopyright.ca or call toll free 1.800.893.5777.

www.pajamapress.ca   info@pajamapress.ca

The publisher gratefully acknowledges the support of the Canada Council for the Arts and the Ontario Arts Council for its publishing program. We acknowledge the financial support of the Government of Canada through the Canada Book Fund (CBF) for our publishing activities.

Library and Archives Canada Cataloguing in Publication
Title: Look up high! Things that fly / Victoria Allenby.
Names: Allenby, Victoria, 1989- author.
Series: Allenby, Victoria, 1989- Big, little concept (Series)
Description: First edition. | Series statement: Big, little concepts
Identifiers: Canadiana 20230218318 | ISBN 9781772782905 (hardcover)
Subjects: LCSH: Flying-machines—Juvenile literature.
Classification: LCC TL547 .A59 2023 | DDC j629.133—dc23

Publisher Cataloging-in-Publication Data (U.S.)
Names: Allenby, Victoria, 1989-, author.
Title: Look up high! Things That Fly / Victoria Allenby.
Description: Toronto, Ontario Canada : Pajama Press, 2023. |Series: Big, Little Concepts, 6. | Summary: "Rhyming text and bright color photographs introduce preschoolers to many kinds of machines that fly. On each spread, a repeating verse is designed to encourage recitation and prediction, while a concluding line names the featured flying machine and introduces a preposition ("The water bomber swoops through the smoke.") A closing spread provides enrichment activities to further a child's engagement with the book and with language skills" – Publisher.
Identifiers: ISBN 978-1-77278-290-5 (hardcover)
Subjects: LCSH: Flight – Juvenile literature. | Aeronautics – Juvenile literature. | Language arts – Juvenile literature. | Stories in rhyme. | BISAC: JUVENILE NONFICTION/Transportation/Aviation. | JUVENILE NONFICTION/Concepts/Words.
Classification: LCC TL547.A5454 |DDC 629.13 – dc23

Cover and book design—Lorena González Guillén
Photographs courtesy of Shutterstock

Manufactured in China by WKT Company

Pajama Press Inc.
11 Davies Avenue, Suite 103, Toronto, Ontario Canada, M4M 2A9

Distributed in Canada by UTP Distribution
5201 Dufferin Street Toronto, Ontario Canada, M3H 5T8

Distributed in the U.S. by Publishers Group West
1 Ingram Blvd. La Vergne, TN 37086, USA